FOOTBALL FUN

by Imogen Kingsley

Raintree is an imprint of Capstone Global Library Limited, a company incorporated in England and Wales having its registered office at 264 Banbury Road, Oxford, OX2 7DY – Registered company number: 6695582

www.raintree.co.uk
myorders@raintree.co.uk

Edited by Shelly Lyons
Designed by Tracy McCabe
Original illustrations © Capstone Global Library Limited 2021
Picture research by Svetlana Zhurkin
Production by Laura Manthe
Originated by Capstone Global Library Ltd
Printed and bound in India

978 1 3982 0336 5 (hardback)
978 1 3982 0335 8 (paperback)

British Library Cataloguing in Publication Data
A full catalogue record for this book is available from the British Library.

Acknowledgements
We would like to thank the following for permission to reproduce photographs: iStockphoto: bonniej, 19; Shutterstock: Aleksandr Lupin, 21, barbsimages, 13, Fafarumba, cover (net), back cover (ball), 1, Fotokostic, 7, irin-k, cover (ball), Kdonmuang, cover (boy), Laszlo Szirtesi, 5, Leonard Zhukovsky, 4, Mandy Godbehear, 8, matimix, 9, Monkey Business Images, 17, muzsy, 14, Paolo Bona, 12, Patty Chan (background), cover, back cover and throughout, Pavel L Photo and Video, 11, Sunny Bright, 15, Susan Leggett, 18, svetalik, cover (grass)

Every effort has been made to contact copyright holders of material reproduced in this book. Any omissions will be rectified in subsequent printings if notice is given to the publisher.

CONTENTS

Words in **bold** are in the glossary.

WHAT IS FOOTBALL?

What is the most popular sport in the world? It's football! Football is played all around the world. In some countries it is called soccer.

Football is played with two teams.

There are 11 players on each team.

Matches take place on a large **pitch**.

The ball is passed around the pitch. Players work together to score goals against the other team.

Players use their feet to kick and pass. They shoot at a goal. The ball hits the back of the net. They score!

The team with the most goals at the end of the match wins.

WHAT DO I NEED TO PLAY?

All you really need to play football is a ball, two goals and some friends. But a few other pieces of **equipment** are helpful.

shin pads

boots

You can wear boots with studs on the bottom. These studs give more grip than trainers or other shoes. Shin pads protect your lower legs from kicks.

WHERE DO I PLAY?

Football can be played on an indoor or outdoor pitch. Children and adults play on different-sized pitches.

The pitch is grass or **turf**. It has white lines. The lines help players know when a ball is in or out of play. There is a goal at each end of the pitch.

HOW DO I PLAY?

A football match starts with a kick-off. The person who makes calls about the rules is the **referee**. The referee blows a whistle to start the match.

referee

Players kick the ball with their feet. They can also bounce the ball off their chests or heads. They can't use their hands or arms to move or catch the ball.

The team with the ball tries to score. To score, a team must get the ball into the other team's goal. The other team tries to block the ball or get it back.

Each team has a **goalkeeper**. This player stands in front of the goal. Goalkeepers must stop the ball from going into the net. They can use their hands to catch or block the ball. They can also use their feet.

HOW CAN I BE A GOOD SPORT?

Football is fun to play when everyone is a good sport! It's important to show good **sportsmanship**. This means being respectful to all players and the referee. It also means listening to your coach.

Being a good sport means you pass the ball. You work together as a team. You cheer for each other too.

When the match is over, the teams shake hands. You all smile and have fun!

SKILL BUILDER: PASSING

Passing the ball is an important skill to master. You can practise passing with these simple steps:

1. You may want to look down at the ball. But you need to look at the pitch first. Find someone to pass the ball to. Or find an open space to pass the ball into.

2. One foot will kick the ball. The other foot will be planted firmly on the ground. This will help you keep your balance.

3. Kick the middle of the ball with the inside part of your foot. Point the toes of your planted foot towards the person you are passing to. It will be easier for your teammate to control the ball if it stays on the ground.

GLOSSARY

equipment tools needed to take part in a sport or activity

goalkeeper player who stays near the goal and tries to keep the ball out of it; a goalkeeper is the only player who can use his or her hands to block or catch a ball

pitch area of grass or turf where football is played

referee person who makes sure all players follow the rules

sportsmanship how a person behaves while playing a sport

turf fake grass

FIND OUT MORE

BOOKS

Football (DK Eyewitness), Hugh Hornby
(DK Children, 2018)

Football (First Sport), James Nixon
(Franklin Watts, 2016)

Messi: From the Playground to the Pitch
(Ultimate Football Heroes), Matt and Tom Oldfield
(Dino Books, 2017)

WEBSITES

www.bbc.co.uk/cbbc/shows/match-of-the-day-kickabout

www.dkfindout.com/uk/sports/football

INDEX